a VIEW from the RIVER

The Chicago Architecture Foundation River Cruise

TEXT BY
Jay Pridmore

PHOTOGRAPHS BY
Hedrich Blessing

Pomegranate

SAN FRANCISCO

DEDICATION

This book is dedicated to the docents of the Chicago Architecture Foundation. Their dedication to learning, generous commitment as volunteers, and most of all, their passion for sharing Chicago's magnificent architecture are an inspiration to us all.

Published by

Pomegranate Communications, Inc.

Box 808022, Petaluma CA 94975

800 227 1428; www.pomegranate.com

Pomegranate Europe Ltd.

Unit 1, Heathcote Business Centre, Hurlbutt Road

Warwick, Warwickshire CV34 6TD, UK

[+44] 0 1926 430111; sales@pomeurope.co.uk

Pomegranate Catalog No. A537

ISBN 978-0-7649-1333-4

Library of Congress Catalog Card Number 00-130347

Cover design by Harrah Argentine

Interior design by Lynn Bell, Monroe Street Studios, Santa Rosa, California

Printed in Korea

14 13 12 11 10 09 08 07 06   16 15 14 13 12 11 10 9 8

Mission

The Chicago Architecture Foundation (CAF) is dedicated to advancing public interest and education in architecture and related design. CAF pursues this mission through a comprehensive program of tours, lectures, exhibitions, special programs, and youth programs, all designed to enhance the public's awareness and appreciation of Chicago's outstanding architectural legacy.

Founded in 1966, the Chicago Architecture Foundation has evolved to become a nationally recognized resource advancing public interest and education in Chicago's outstanding architecture. Its programs serve more than three hundred fifty thousand people each year. For more information contact us at the address below or visit us on our website:

Chicago Architecture Foundation
224 South Michigan Avenue
Chicago, IL 60604
312-922-TOUR
www.architecture.org

Contents

ACKNOWLEDGMENTS

This book was inspired by the Chicago Architecture Foundation's River Cruise, one of the city's most popular cultural attractions. The Foundation's purpose in telling the story of Chicago architecture and its expertise in describing the buildings have made the River Cruise an educational pleasure for natives of Chicago and tourists alike.

Many individuals helped produce this book. Most important in laying the groundwork were the people who make the River Cruise possible, the Foundation's volunteer docents. These men and women lead tours and tell stories that make Chicago's buildings as fascinating to hear about as they are impressive to behold. Docent and tour director Robert Irving authored the docents' guide, from which much of the information here has been adapted. Others whose research is reflected in this text are Judith Randall and Tori Simms.

The splendid photographs gracing these pages are the work of Hedrich Blessing, one of the nation's leading firms specializing in architectural photography. Jack Hedrich, Mike Houlahan, and Bob

Shimer showed infinite interest in this book, and the images reflect their understanding of Chicago architecture and their dedication to conveying it to the public.

The staff of the Chicago Architecture Foundation also took this book in loving hand. President Lynn Osmond, Vice-President of Programs and Tours Bonita Mall, board member Henry Kuehn, and staff members Bill Burrows, Ellen Christensen, Dan Dorsey, Leanne Eben, Zurich Esposito, Barbara Hrbek, Steve Majsak, Mark Millmore, and Dave Woollard did much to help move the project from conception to completion.

Thanks are due as well to Edward C. Hirschland, whose skillful administration and shaping of the book were enhanced by his boundless appreciation of the subject, and to Larry Okrent, whose map is a vital complement to the text. Finally, thanks go to Katie Burke and James Donnelly of Pomegranate, who skillfully assembled the pieces and attended to the details, creating a book of which we hope Chicago is proud.

Jay Pridmore
Chicago, December 1999

INTRODUCTION

Chicago's reputation as one of the world's centers of architecture can be traced back to the years immediately following the Chicago Fire of 1871. Chicago was already the hub of the American Midwest when thousands of the nation's most ambitious men and women converged on the city to help rebuild it.

By the mid-nineteenth century, with the opening of the Illinois and Michigan Canal and the arrival of the railroad, Chicago's location on Lake Michigan and its ready access to the heartland of America made the city vital to the nation's economy. Trade and industry made Chicago grow as very few cities have grown. Hence came the pressing need to build the city quickly—especially after the Fire—making maximum practical use of relatively confined downtown commercial lots. Chicago's distinctive solution to this challenge came in the form of the tall, compact, metal-framed buildings that began emerging in the Loop, planned by such pathbreaking architects as William Le Baron Jenney, Louis Sullivan, and John Wellborn Root. The many great architects who followed them created commercial and public buildings that set new standards for engineering efficiency and aesthetic quality.

Over many years, the Loop has developed into a vibrant living museum of architecture. And it is no coincidence that the Chicago River, which courses through the heart of the city, provides an ideal tour of that museum. When the Chicago Architecture Foundation's Architecture River Cruise was inaugurated in 1984, it instantly became popular as a way to see striking skyscrapers in full profile and to hear marvelous stories about the people who built them. No wonder the River Cruise is today one of the city's most popular cultural attractions.

In this book are captured many of the striking images and fascinating stories that delight the more than 100,000 people who take the cruise each year. Whether you are just beginning your exploration of Chicago architecture or are refining your knowledge as an enthusiast, we think you will enjoy this book—and our tour. And we hope you will remind anyone you know who is planning a visit to Chicago that the best way to gain a grasp of the city's history is to explore its world-famous buildings.

Welcome to Chicago. Enjoy its inspiring architecture!

Lynn J. Osmond
President, Chicago Architecture Foundation

Docent Acknowledgments

The CAF wishes to recognize the following individuals for their outstanding contribution to the success of the Architecture River Cruise in 2002. Their dedication and enthusiasm helped make the CAF cruise the number-one rated visitor experience in Chicago.

Chicago Architecture Foundation

2002 Architecture River Cruise Docents

Helen Albert	Bill Hinchliff	Nancy Nusser
Peg Albert	Harry Hirsch	Bobbi Pinkert
Doug Anderson	Bob Irving	Mary Plauché
Jurgis Anysas	Bennett Johnson	Judith Randall
Geoffrey Baer	Gina Johnson	David Redemske
Alice Blum	Eric Kille	Tom Reynolds
Deborah Carey	Mili Kirsh	Maureen Sauvé
John Chaput	Art Kruski	Pauline Scharres
Henry Cohen	Blossom Levin	Sydney Schuler
Syma Dodson	Helen Lewis	Polly Sippy
Sylvia Dunbeck	Jill Lowe	Chuck Solomonson
Craig Easly	Brian Lozell	Hy Speck
Karen Flannery	Karen Luckritz	Marie Spicuzza
Debra Jean Frels	Mary Ludgin	Bronwein Stevens
Karen Genelly	Aileen Mandel	Diane Stone
Linda Goggin	Jordan Marsh	Donald Wiberg
Ed Goltz	Gail Matejcic	Joyce Wiberg
Louise Haack	Bill Myers	Barbara Zink
Joy Hebert	Sally Nochowitz	

The CAF also wishes to recognize the contribution to the success of the Architecture River Cruise made by Holly and Bob Agra and the staff and pilots of *Chicago's First Lady* and *Chicago's Little Lady*.

Pictured is Henry Cohen, a Chicago Architecture Foundation docent, conducting the River Cruise tour on *Chicago's First Lady*.

Most of America's great rivers have been carved by the slow forces of nature. But the profile of the Chicago River, as striking as any of the world's waterways, was wrought largely by human device. Its flow was determined by engineers, and its canyon walls designed by architects. Yet its splendor is real and its sheer majesty has become one of the city's great natural resources.

Certainly, the Chicago River lacked beauty when the first Europeans found it. The river called Checagou, named by Native Americans after a wild onion that grew here, moved lazily toward the lake and seemed more a marsh than a river. Early visitors found the place unpromising. Noted as excellent ground for mosquitoes and mud, it seemed up close like a good place to avoid.

In the grander scheme of things, however, Chicago was blessed. In 1673, French explorers Jacques Marquette and Louis Jolliet discovered that this river represented the critical link between the Great Lakes and the riches of America's interior. A portage of less than a mile separated the South Branch of the Chicago River from the Des Plaines River, which flowed to the Illinois, thence to the Mississippi. This was well understood in 1803 when the United States government built Fort Dearborn near the spot where Lake Michigan met the river.

Chicago's destiny was sealed in 1828 when the Illinois legislature resolved to build a canal, which fostered great hope that this would become the hub of the nation's Northwest. A land boom ensued, followed by occasional busts. But the trends favored those who had faith in this village and this river. A lot that was purchased for $100 in 1832 went for $15,000 just three years later.

For most people, however, getting wealth out of Chicago and its river required hard work. Sandbars had long impeded passage of any but the smallest boats into the river's safe harbor. In the 1830s, therefore, soldiers built jetties and dredged a channel to admit sailing vessels filled with food, building materials, and people. By the 1850s, with the banks of the river lined with wharves, Chicago became a trading center of national scope. Grain elevators and fresh-cut lumber stacked on docks constituted Chicago's skyline and dwarfed the buildings that were going up all around.

With abundant lumber, balloon-frame construction evolved in Chicago as nowhere else. Employing two-by-fours and nails, balloon frames were historically important; not only did they enable the village to grow with blazing speed, but they also made Chicago a tinderbox. As destiny unfolded, the Chicago Fire of 1871 destroyed the city and ignited a rebuilding phase that become one of the most architecturally fertile periods in history.

As agriculture developed in the heartland, grain became the great commodity of Chicago and its river. Elevators went up all along the banks—built in brick after the Fire, and so highly mechanized in some cases that *Scientific American* carried detailed engravings of the automated systems that operated inside.

The greatest engineering feat connected to the Chicago River remains the reversal of its flow. Again, this was born of necessity, the need to carry urban sewage away from Lake Michigan and relieve "an abominable condition of filth beyond the power of the pen to describe," according to one report in the latter part of the century.

In 1900, the Sanitary and Ship Canal connected the Chicago and Illinois Rivers with a channel sufficiently wide and deep to pull water from the North and Main Branches southward. This created hard feelings in St. Louis, naturally, where they felt that the engineering marvel in Chicago was a sanitation nightmare for them.

But chemists proved to federal judges that bacteria would be oxidized away by the time the sewage reached St. Louis, and one of the "engineering wonders of the United States," as it was called many years later, was a reality.

The reversal of the river did more to clean the lake than the river. Nor did the river benefit initially from the civic virtue that kept the lakefront "forever open, clear and free," as mandated by an early municipal ordinance. That began to change with the Plan of Chicago of 1909, the great architect Daniel Burnham's grand scheme for the Midwest metropolis. Burnham envisioned broad boulevards extending along both sides of the river, connected to a grand lakefront with beautiful piers, and a civic center to rival the Place de la Concord in Paris. This reflected a trend called the City Beautiful movement. A classical-style city center would generate civic pride and attract private investment.

Cooperation was not immediate. Typical of riverfront residents were the railroads, with tracks and depots everywhere. The Illinois Central sprawled on the south bank by the lake. The Chicago & Northwestern webbed Wolf Point, where the Merchandise Mart now sits. On the South Branch, a broad bend which dis-

When this engraving was made in 1866, the Chicago River was the bustling city's main artery. Sailing vessels crowded the wharves to unload lumber, grain, and another vital import: people. Early railroads serving the vast American West emanated from the banks of the Chicago River, helping turn this once-unprepossessing stream into one of the nation's most important waterways.

AN EVER-CHANGING SKYLINE

The great curved tower of 333 West Wacker Drive fills one of the most prominent sites on the Chicago River, the junction of the South and Main Branches. It is well loved mainly because of the many ways it reflects the sky and the surrounding skyline. Great buildings have the ability to change with new needs. This one changes with the weather.

rupted the urban grid was lined by a tangle of other railroad interests that refused for years to straighten things out.

But in small steps, the river has been improved. Wacker Drive was built in 1926. The South Branch was straightened in 1930. Slowly, architects used the river as a design element, now viewed as an aesthetic and not just an economic amenity.

The transformation of the Chicago River has been a long process, but an accelerating one. Environmentalism opened the city's eyes to the river's potential, and by the 1980s, planners imagined a continuous series of walkways on the river's edge from Roosevelt Road on the South Branch all the way around to the lake and Navy Pier. Despite difficult logistics and expense, some architects and developers have succeeded in realizing significant stretches of the Riverwalk.

Boat traffic, meanwhile, has increased. A shuttle between Michigan Avenue and commuter trains has enjoyed modest success. Pleasure boat traffic has expanded greatly, especially in tours conducted by the Chicago Architecture Foundation, which discovered some years ago that the river is one of the world's most spectacular "museums" of architecture.

Today, the Chicago River represents urban evolution of the most positive kind. Builders who once ignored the river now use it as an integral part of their designs. A natural resource that once served strict economic utility now brings Chicagoans seeking relaxation. And the plans laid by Daniel Burnham nearly a century ago have created what is now a national monument and cultural icon wrought by sustained ingenuity and Chicago's indomitable will.

Great Lakes Building, 1912

Holabird & Roche

123 North Wacker Drive, 1988

Perkins & Will

In the 1980s, many new buildings were designed to be "contextual," blending harmoniously with the existing, often historical architectural environment. This riverscape reveals layers of Chicago history. The red brick Great Lakes Building by Holabird & Roche charmingly reflects the sense of proportion that was a hallmark of the Chicago School. Standing behind it is Perkins & Will's 123 North Wacker, which combines features of stone-clad skyscrapers—including a rooftop pyramid like the one on the Civic Opera Building downriver—with sheer glass walls that are a trademark of the classic modernist tower.

CHICAGO'S SKYSCRAPERS

The city's earliest commercial buildings are all but obscured today. But the later, taller, more glimmering urban towers that rise from the edge of the Chicago River owe an immense debt to Chicago's early commercial builders whose art evolved in the twenty years after the Fire from traditional masonry-wall construction to something new, called the skyscraper.

Skyscrapers began in a most utilitarian way. In 1885, the Home Insurance Building in the Loop was regarded as the world's first at nine stories, later raised to eleven. Architect William Le Baron Jenney designed it; as a Civil War engineer, he understood bridge construction and imagined that he could build a tall building with a metal frame. When Jenney wrapped the Home Insurance Building with a non-load-bearing curtain wall, it was hardly an artistic statement. Jenney's objective was to build rapidly—metal went up faster than masonry—and increase floor space. In the process, he started a revolution in architecture.

The skyscraper quickly advanced in technology and in style. Some architects worked out problems in anchoring the pylons in Chicago's damp and sandy soil. Others used steel frames to open great windows for abundant natural light. Chicago's influential architect Louis Sullivan asserted that skyscrapers represented a truly indigenous American building style, and he analyzed the ideal "tripartite" skyscraper by its parts—base, shaft, and capital—a solid base, a soaring midsection, and a romantic if not ethereal rooftop. "Every inch a proud and soaring thing," he proclaimed, was the desired result.

History and economic necessity have sustained Chicago as the world's center of the skyscraper. And just as other American rivers reveal layers of geology and natural history, the canyon walls of the Chicago River exhibit a slice of the architectural past rarely visible in such a vivid tableau. From the old Chicago School through Beaux-Arts, Art Deco, modernism, and postmodernism, the river does more than tell an important story. It is a living museum of architecture and a historical treasure as inspiring as it is articulate.

BOEING WORLD HEADQUARTERS, 1990

Perkins & Will

Designed by Ralph Johnson of Perkins & Will, Boeing World Headquarters (formally Morton International Building) evokes early European modernism. Walkways offer a view of the river's three branches. To accommodate railroads below, a large part of the building is suspended from the bridgelike structure on top.

THE MODERNIST PLAN

When it was conceived in the late 1960s, Illinois Center was recognized as one of the largest urban development projects ever undertaken. The initial plans by Mies van der Rohe included an orderly scheme integrating skyscrapers and open spaces. After Mies's death his successor firm, Fujikawa, Conterato, Lohan & Associates, developed and carried out the rest of the plan, most of which was realized in the 1970s.

3 CHICAGO'S BRIDGES

As it grew, Chicago became a city of bridges, though there were always ship captains who complained that they snarled the river. The first bridge across the river was at Dearborn Street and the second at Clark. These were "float bridges," with pivots at one end, floating pontoons at the other, and ropes to pull them open and closed. In the early 1850s, a new type, a "swing bridge," was built at Clark Street with a central pier on which the entire span could turn. This was an improved technology, but left two narrow channels instead of one wide one, and ship captains did not mind ramming the pier to make a statement against impeded traffic.

Lift bridges and drawbridges were the answer, and Chicago soon became home to more movable bridges than any other city in the world, and so many types that the city is now regarded as a "museum of bridges." But by 1900, engineers had discovered the type that would dominate bridge building in Chicago for the entire century: the "bascule trunnion." *Bascule* is French for see-saw, and the principle is just that. As each leaf tips up on its fulcrum or trunnion, the short end (on the shore side) is counterweighted so carefully that an electric motor of relatively small size can lift a span of thousands of tons with ease.

Swing bridges, such as this one at Lake Street in 1866, were sturdier than float bridges, but they made passage for larger boats difficult.

Facing the Water

Quaker Tower, the Westin River North Hotel, and Marina City all were designed to provide striking views of the city from within and to be admired in profile from a distance.

THE NORTH BANK

The renaissance of the Chicago River and its role as an important public space are relatively new. But the river has long served architects as an inspired complement to their designs—such as the IBM Building and the Chicago Sun-Times Building.

21

City of Bridges

The river affords some of the greatest views of Chicago. At night the city's powerful profile and ceaseless energy are on dazzling display.

VIEW FROM THE BRIDGE

Michigan Avenue at the Chicago River has long served as a vital nucleus of Chicago's development. In 1803, high ground on the south bank became the site of Fort Dearborn, a remote federal garrison to secure a promising trade route. When the inland canal was built in the 1840s and promise turned into commerce, warehouses quickly lined the river's banks.

There was no Michigan Avenue Bridge in those days; it was more important to keep the channel free and clear. On either side were warehouses and factories, notably the McCormick Reaper Works where the Tribune Tower now stands, and the railroads that served them. But in 1909 Daniel Burnham's Plan of Chicago stressed the importance of Michigan Avenue, which then ran south. His plan was to widen it and extend it north over the river.

Burnham imagined that "Michigan Avenue is probably destined to carry the heaviest move-ment of any street in the world." He never saw it come true, but Charles Wacker, who succeeded Burnham as planning czar and assumed the chairmanship of the Chicago Plan Commission, campaigned hard for Michigan Avenue's connecting link. Finally completed in 1920, "the mighty two level bridge, which rose in the air like an alligator's jaws," as journalist Lloyd Lewis wrote, was opened.

Burnham's advice had been to "make no little plans," and Chicago followed. The Michigan Avenue Bridge inspired a decade of major developments for Chicago. The Magnificent Mile began going up piece by piece. Wacker Drive, completed in 1926, transformed a neighborhood that was once cramped and industrial into something proud, expansive, and custom-made for self-assured capitalists and the skyscrapers they built.

WRIGLEY BUILDING, 1921 (NORTH ADDITION COMPLETED 1924)

Graham, Anderson, Probst & White

Begun before the Michigan Avenue Bridge was built, the Wrigley Building was a powerful expression of confidence in the city's future. America's leading chewing gum manufacturer chose Chicago's most prominent architecture firm at the time, Graham, Anderson, Probst & White, to produce a dazzling landmark where dark warehouses once stood.

The design is Beaux-Arts, with garlands of French "renaissance" ornament all around and a tower modeled after the Giralda Tower in Seville, Spain. But there are modern architectural conceptions at play here, too. Given the angle of the river and an irregular site, the architects made a virtue of necessity by creating not one but two large facades, meant to dominate any view of the area. Both the first section of the Wrigley Building and the north addition, which went up three years later, were sheathed with white-glazed terra-cotta, a then-popular material that could be brilliantly illuminated at night.

The tower's observation deck was once the highest point in Chicago, and visitors came by the carload to take in the "airplane view" of the city and the land beyond. The Wrigley Building remains a favorite among Chicagoans, not because it is architecturally advanced but because of its exuberant assertiveness and splendor.

TRIBUNE TOWER, 1925

Howells & Hood

The Tribune Tower Competition of 1922 proved to be a turning point in modern architecture—but in an indirect way. When the owners of the *Chicago Tribune* announced that a $100,000 prize would be awarded for the winning design to produce "the most beautiful and distinctive office building in the world," more than 250 entries flooded in from around the world, representing styles that ranged from ancient Egyptian to Bauhaus-modern. The commission ultimately went to the New York firm headed by John Mead Howells and Raymond Hood. The building, with its elaborate, ornamented Gothic-revival tower modeled in part after Rouen Cathedral in France, was completed in 1925. But as things turned out, the second-place entry, by the Finnish architect Eliel Saarinen, made a deeper impression than the Howells & Hood building. Although Saarinen's plan also was Gothic in profile, it was relatively unadorned, with a series of narrow stone piers angling skyward like lightning bolts. Nonetheless, the Tribune Tower as built became one of Chicago's most readily recognized buildings. Together with the Wrigley Building across the street, it forms a gateway to the Magnificent Mile.

CHICAGO TRIBUNE TOWER COMPETITION ENTRY, 1922

Eliel Saarinen

In the Tribune Tower Competition of 1922, this entry by the Finnish architect Eliel Saarinen took second place; it was never built. Nevertheless, it was widely admired and exerted a deep and enduring influence on architecture. Saarinen's tower appeared to be the quintessentially American skyscraper, beholden to no historical precedent and symbolic of the young nation's power. An elderly Louis Sullivan, who had designed some of Chicago's earliest skyscrapers, recognized that Saarinen "grasped the intricate problems of the lofty steel-framed structure, the significance of its origins, and held the solution unwaveringly in mind, in such wise no American architect has as yet shown the required depth of thought and steadfastness of purpose to achieve." Many American architects emulated Saarinen's design in skyscrapers of the 1920s (see Holabird & Root's 333 North Michigan), and its form is still echoed in recently built commercial office towers.

CHICAGO SUN-TIMES BUILDING, 1957

Naess & Murphy

The view from the Michigan Avenue Bridge continues to change as the years pass. In this photo the R. R. Donnelley Center, completed in 1992, is not yet present. The river was changing in 1957, too, when the Chicago Sun-Times Building (right) was built in black granite, aluminum, and glass. Its architecture, with touches of modern styling, is largely utilitarian. The newspaper's printing press is visible behind a lower band of ribbon windows, and a rail siding for newsprint runs underneath. A small plaza beside the Sun-Times Building was added not on the river but close to it, as modern architects sought ways to make the riverfront as well as their office buildings user-friendly.

333 NORTH MICHIGAN AVENUE, 1928

Holabird & Root

LONDON GUARANTEE AND ACCIDENT BUILDING, 1923

Alfred S. Alschuler

The intersection of the Chicago River and Michigan Avenue was already the architectural anchor of downtown Chicago when the office of Holabird & Root designed 333 North Michigan Avenue. Reflecting the influence of Saarinen's second-place entry in the Tribune Tower competition, it is a modern classic among Chicago skyscrapers. Stripped to its elegant basics, it represents many elements of the Sullivanesque ideal. The base is sumptuous, and the narrow profile is functional, assuring an interior filled with light. In its early years, the building had many architects as tenants, attracted not only by the advanced architecture but also by the Tavern Club on the top floor, an exclusive speakeasy. The club was adorned with modernist murals that depicted mythical subjects, "symbolizing, perhaps, that thought as well as pleasure is a part of the Tavern's ideals," wrote architect John Root, a charter member.

Across the avenue, the London Guarantee Building is of another generation, though it was built only five years earlier. The focus of its five-story base is a grand entrance flanked by Corinthian columns, and the building's upper section bears a classical colonnade, a balustraded cornice, and a domed pavilion at the very top. The same unabashed neoclassical emphasis, echoing the Beaux-Arts preferences of the City Beautiful movement, is evident in the nearby bridge houses, with their dramatic bas-reliefs depicting scenes from Chicago's past, such as the Fort Dearborn Massacre of 1812 and the rebuilding of the city after the Fire.

JEWELERS BUILDING, 1926

Giaver & Dinkelberg with Thielbar & Fugard

ONE EAST WACKER DRIVE, 1962

Shaw, Metz & Associates

Wacker Drive, completed in 1926, accomplished precisely what Daniel Burnham and Charles Wacker intended. It inspired ambitious and at times noble architecture all along the banks of the river. Although not every tower on the boulevard stands as a Chicago classic, each one clearly reflects the moment in the city's architectural history when it was produced. The Jewelers Building rose as a Beaux-Arts dream when two former members of Burnham's office, Joachim Giaver and Frederick Dinkelberg, designed an office building with a modern interior (including an elevator-equipped twenty-two-story auto garage) and a terra-cotta exterior decked with neo-baroque ornament and classical pavilions overhead.

One East Wacker Drive (formerly the United of America Building) was of a different age—designed by Alfred Shaw, who designed the Merchandise Mart and other Art Deco buildings when he worked for Graham, Anderson, Probst & White in the twenties. By the 1960s, Shaw's style had evolved into pure modernism, characterized by soaring towers stripped to their bare essentials—such as this one, the tallest marble-clad building in the world when it went up in 1962.

LINCOLN TOWER, 1928

Herbert H. Riddle

HOTEL 71, 1958

Milton Schwartz

The historical and the modern live in harmony with the neo-gothic Lincoln Tower tucked between the classical London Guarantee Building and the glassy Hotel 71 (formerly known as Executive House). Rising to forty-two floors, the octagonal Lincoln Tower was briefly, in 1928, Chicago's tallest structure. It remains one of the narrowest skyscrapers anywhere—just nine and a half feet across at the top. Not surprisingly, it required a steel frame of extraordinary strength to enable it to resist Chicago's notoriously mighty winds.

By 1958, when Hotel 71 was built, tastes and styles had changed. Yet with "ribbon" windows wrapping its corners and its overall lightness, this building—like Lincoln Tower—emphasizes the strength of its steel skeleton.

5 THE CHICAGO SCHOOL

The Chicago School of Architecture began with the burst of commercial building that followed the Great Chicago Fire of 1871. It brought architects by the hundreds, each one seeking commissions that valued economy above all. Thus, the successful ones devised rectangular plans, because they filled their lots, and engineered steel frames because those went up quickly; they also included large windows to flood working interiors with plenty of natural light.

These were practical buildings. But their architects, many trained in classicism, were deeply inspired by a city of unprecedented power. Chicago deserved buildings of practicality and grandeur, they said, and men like William Le Baron Jenney, John Holabird, Martin Roche, and Louis Sullivan designed buildings of distinction, invented the form-follows-function canon, and discovered a new kind of architectural beauty.

Some embellished windows and doors with Romanesque arches, Gothic roof lines, and intricate carving in the spaces between the windows. But Chicago architecture came to celebrate the pure function of downtown stores, riverfront warehouses, and Loop office buildings. When architects from Europe visited Chicago, they marveled at the elegant simplicity of the Chicago loft. It contributed significantly to their ideas of modernity.

There are few Chicago School buildings left on the river, and most of them don't face the water. But their legacy is everywhere. The loft's straightforward lines guided the streamlined era of the twenties. Its love of large interior space influenced the modernist glass towers of the postwar era. And today, architects combing the past for styles to weave into the future find that the big-shouldered architecture of the nineteenth century is a recognized American classic.

Montgomery Ward & Co., 1908

Schmidt, Garden & Martin
(Administration Building, 1930, Willis J. McCauley; corporate headquarters, 1974, Minoru Yamasaki & Associates)

Montgomery Ward's mail-order business was expanding enormously around the turn of the century, so the firm needed an office-and-distribution center of great size and efficiency. Schmidt, Garden & Martin readily complied, producing a simple, highly functional warehouse that was, when it opened, the world's largest reinforced concrete structure (left). By following the curve of the river, the architects emphasized the expansive character of the warehouse and of the Montgomery Ward enterprise. This effect is enhanced by the Art Deco–style Administration Building (right, behind bridge), just south of Chicago Avenue. Its corner tower is capped with a sixteen-foot-tall sculpture titled *The Spirit of Progress*. Behind (top right) is the 1974 corporate headquarters designed by Minoru Yamasaki & Associates.

37

HELENE CURTIS BUILDING, 1912

L. Gustav Hallberg
(renovated 1984, Booth/Hansen & Associates)

One of the most prominent Chicago School examples left on the river, this building exhibits a classic if modest form. Columns and spandrels are without ornamentation. The structure's charm lies in its honest expression of the simple steel frame that supports it. Its simple arrangement of base, shaft, and capital is unprepossessing but gives the building added presence. The use of modern glass in the 1984 renovation, here in progress, highlights the solidity of this enduring reminder of Chicago's past. The Wells Street Bridge, which runs beside the Curtis Building, is another solid piece of design. Elevated-transit trains use its top deck. When it opened in 1922, it was the longest double-deck span (268 feet between trunnions) in the world.

REID, MURDOCH AND COMPANY BUILDING, 1913

George C. Nimmons

QUAKER TOWER, 1987

Skidmore, Owings & Merrill

WESTIN RIVER NORTH HOTEL, 1987

Helmuth, Obata & Kassabaum; Takayama & Associates

In the Reid, Murdoch and Company warehouse (above) architect George Nimmons did something new, orienting the building toward the river at a time when most buildings turned their backs on it. As in his 1906 Sears, Roebuck complex on the city's West Side, he employed Arts and Crafts styling and wrapped a delicate skin of brick around columns and arches, and around the tower that contains the building's water tank and sprinkler system—contributing graceful notes to an otherwise simple, straightforward commercial edifice.

Quaker Tower (photograph opposite page, second from left), a purely modernist building designed by the firm of Skidmore, Owings & Merrill, is another essentially conventional building that exhibits an uncommon respect for the Chicago River. Inside, the lobby seems to flow out beyond its glass walls toward the river and the Clark Street Bridge, with its elegant pony-truss design from 1929.

The Westin Hotel (third from left) was originally the Nikko Hotel. Its riverside restaurants blended indoor and outdoor elements. A few years after the hotel opened, Japanese architect Kenzo Tange was commissioned to design a Japanese-inspired garden on the south bank directly across the river.

6 ART DECO SKYSCRAPERS

The completion of Wacker Drive in 1926 in the midst of unprecedented prosperity triggered feverish construction in the Roaring Twenties. Many of the river's finest buildings, and once its tallest, rose up in this lively decade with the streamlined thrust of Art Deco.

When the decade began, architects and clients were still attached to historical styles, as in the Wrigley Building and Tribune Tower. But modernism was in the air, from the Bauhaus in Germany, for example, and Le Corbusier in France. In Chicago, where Louis Sullivan taught that "form follows function" in tall office buildings, architects grew impatient with thick blankets of ornamentation.

The result was stripped-down, streamlined skyscrapers. Like Saarinen's never-built Tribune Tower project, these buildings soared upward with emphatic vertical power, unimpeded by cornices and capitals. Of Chicago's leading architectural firms, Holabird & Root was most committed to the streamlined modern look, with "setback" skyscrapers shooting skyward in stepped-back sections. This design cut a striking figure against the sky while also adhering to a Chicago ordinance, passed in 1923, against sheer walls so high as to block all natural light.

Graham, Anderson, Probst & White also advanced the modernist cause. As the firm was the successor to Daniel Burnham, Graham, Anderson had a harder time resisting classical overlays. But they too designed soaring setback skyscrapers like the Opera House and streamlined masterpieces like the Merchandise Mart. Their interiors could be traditional, but rarely without the color and flowing space that were hallmarks of the modern era in architecture.

DAILY NEWS BUILDING (ONE NORTH RIVERSIDE PLAZA), 1929

Holabird & Root

This might be the mightiest edifice of its kind in Chicago. It thrusts skyward with a kind of inevitability, an effect produced by its angular rhythm and sharp contrasts of light and shadow—both keynotes of Art Deco architecture. Although this is a building that signifies power, it also has a reposed, even calming quality— "sphinxlike," as one writer aptly observed.

In addition, the design includes an imaginative and graceful solution to an unusual technical problem. This was the first Chicago building constructed on railroad air rights, specifically those associated with tracks running north from Union Station. The architects devised a system of pylons to raise the building over the rail yard and a sophisticated expansion chamber and smokestack to siphon off diesel fumes. The design also includes a broad plaza that faces the Civic Opera Building across the river. The result is a triumphant blending of skilled engineering and pleasing urban design.

43

LaSalle-Wacker Building, 1930

Holabird & Root

Builders Building, 1927

Graham, Anderson, Probst & White
(addition, 1986, Skidmore, Owings & Merrill)

Like many skyscrapers of the period, the LaSalle-Wacker Building (left) assumes the "armchair" form—a high "back" placed between two "arms"—for optimal light and ventilation. Designed by Holabird & Root along with the Chicago modernist Andrew Rebori, this office building was up-to-date in every way. The lobby was stylized with polished metal and etched glass. The elevators boasted "push-button control," and the offices were wired for interoffice phones and buzzer systems.

Created as a showplace for the construction industry, the Builders Building was designed by Graham, Anderson, Probst & White in what was then an almost aggressively conservative style. Although its 1988 addition (right) is also unremarkable, the two sections of the building jointly emphasize several enduring architectural values. On both sides, classical proportion projects strength, as does the Sullivanesque "tri-partite" skyscraper, with its base, shaft, and capital. The result is a structure that is elegant, compelling, and proof that restraint is rewarded in the long run.

MERCHANDISE MART, 1930

Graham, Anderson, Probst & White

Conceived as a grandiose symbol as well as a profit-generating enterprise, the Merchandise Mart was built by Marshall Field and Company as America's "Great Central Market," a facility where dry-goods merchandising would be centralized and modernized. Built on the air rights of the old Chicago & North Western terminal, the Mart was intended to attract wholesale firms by the hundreds and wholesale customers from all over the country. The building was envisioned as a shining example of urban planning as well. Its riverfront entrance was designed as the first stretch of the projected North Bank Drive, a mirror image of Wacker Drive across the river.

The Depression blunted many of these grand-scale plans. After World War II the vast complex was sold to Joseph P. Kennedy, who attracted corporate tenants and also developed the Mart as a furnishing-design center. Through its commercial ups and downs, the Merchandise Mart has stood as one of Chicago's most ambitious pieces of architecture. It has the mass of an overgrown Chicago School commercial building. It has the streamlined detail of an Art Deco skyscraper. The Mart also features the giant display windows and colorful interiors of a stylish department store.

The Merchandise Mart continues to change. The Kennedy family sold the building in 1998. Two of its longtime tenants—Quaker Oats and NBC—now have buildings of their own on the river. But the Mart's location has only improved with age, and its interior—which features murals by Jules Guérin, who illustrated Daniel Burnham's 1909 Plan of Chicago—was recently restored to its Art Deco splendor.

CIVIC OPERA BUILDING, 1929

Graham, Anderson, Probst & White

With its soaring, armchair-like profile, Chicago's skyscraping opera house, commissioned by the ambitious utilities tycoon Samuel Insull, quickly earned the nickname "Insull's throne." In fact, the building was anything but aristocratic. It was created as a multiuse structure, with rented office spaces taking up most of the floors above the theater. And while the auditorium was designed to be the most expansive and splendid anywhere, it contained not a single elevated private box where the elite might exhibit themselves to the proletariat. Thus did this grand theater reflect Chicago's fiercely democratic self-image.

Among Chicago's many claims to architectural fame, this was the city where the materials of glass and steel spawned the doctrine of "less is more." Modernism is present everywhere along the river, in the classic forms of Mies van der Rohe, the skyscrapers of his followers, and even in the buildings designed by architects who professed to be dissenters.

The development of the modernist skyscraper is a complex story, but its critical moment came in 1938 when Ludwig Mies van der Rohe, formerly head of the modernist Bauhaus school of Germany, left his homeland and moved to Chicago. The Bauhaus school had long sought a marriage of industry and art. Mies meanwhile conceptualized an architecture stripped to its bare essentials—skeleton, skin, and the space inside.

In America, Mies found the technology to execute his dream—the glass-and-steel tower—and his influence on architecture was instantaneous. A "Miesian" skyscraper, architects found, was pure and even ethereal. His Lake Shore Drive apartment towers, and later designs including the IBM Building on the river, had classic proportions, a complex play of light on the surface, and virtually no extraneous decoration.

The Chicago-based firm of Skidmore, Owings & Merrill, with many students of Mies in its employ, was destined to become the most prolific designer of corporate buildings in postwar America. SOM, as it is now called, applied the philosophy of modernism to large projects—combining the "less is more" of Mies with the "make no little plans" of Daniel Burnham. The firm distinguished itself by blending cutting-edge architecture with advanced engineering, a marriage that brought forth buildings of such fame as the Sears Tower.

There were always dissenters to the modernists, and in Chicago the most notable among them was Bertrand Goldberg, who designed the circular twin towers of Marina City in the rectilinear 1960s. Goldberg had studied with Mies in Germany but found his architecture inhospitable. While Goldberg, too, searched for a modern formula, he concluded that balconies for barbecues in the city were more important than the play of light off glassy surfaces.

By the 1980s, rebellion against the modernists was in full force, with the postmodernists substituting historical ironies—such as Philip Johnson's Chippendale-style tower for AT&T in Manhattan—for plain severity. But postmodernism ran its course, and as architects continue to search the past for new ideas, hardly anyone forgets the glass tower of yore. New buildings in Chicago come with classical touches, Art Deco lines, even Prairie School profiles. But rarely do they appear without the glimmer of glass that makes buildings appear animate, and some even to move.

GATEWAY CENTER I (RIGHT) AND II, 1965 AND 1968

Skidmore, Owings & Merrill

The Chicago River's earliest "renaissance" occurred in a place that is little seen by most Chicagoans, the west side of the South Branch, where there was room to create a long, unbroken esplanade. In the early 1960s, Tishman Realty purchased air rights over a long stretch of the Union Station rail yard and hired Skidmore, Owings & Merrill to redevelop an area that had chiefly served as a gateway to skid row. Plans to consolidate the rail terminals and create a major transportation center there did not materialize.

51

SEARS TOWER, 1974

Skidmore, Owings & Merrill

311 SOUTH WACKER DRIVE, 1990

Kohn Pedersen Fox

Completed in 1974, the Sears Tower, with its assertive stepped-back silhouette and sheathing of black aluminum and bronze-tinted glass, continues to set the standard among modern-day skyscrapers. Standing 110 stories and only recently surpassed as the world's tallest building—in 1996 by Petronas Towers in Kuala Lumpur, Malaysia—it achieves its majestic presence through a design founded on nine framed "contiguous tubes," each 75 feet square, that are banded together to supply lateral strength and resist Chicago's notorious winds. The building reflects its architects' exceptional grasp of materials, loads, and proportion.

The Sears Tower's Skydeck has become a mecca for tourists. The famous building also attracts daredevils who have scaled its exterior. Other architects, however, have steered clear and not challenged it. Other glass towers, no matter how finely wrought, could hardly compete with Sears's sheer size—which is certainly what Kohn Pedersen Fox concluded in their design for 311 South Wacker Drive, which stands next door. In the shadow of the Sears Tower, they built what was in 1990 the world's tallest reinforced concrete building. This is a postmodern extravaganza. The architects crowned it with a huge glass cylinder that is brilliantly illuminated at night.

Marina City, 1967

Bertrand Goldberg Associates

IBM Building, 1971

Office of Mies van der Rohe with C. F. Murphy Associates

Marina City and the IBM Building represent one of modernism's more meaningful "conversations" on the riverfront. IBM (right) was Mies van der Rohe's final skyscraper in Chicago, and it demonstrates the subtle effect of solid steel, reflective glass, and dark shadow. Next door are the twin towers of Marina City, designed by Bertrand Goldberg, who as a young man had studied under Mies at the Bauhaus.

Goldberg's objective in Marina City was to help breathe life and warmth into a downtown that had grown desolate after dark in the wake of years of burgeoning suburban growth. It was designed as a multiuse complex, with facilities for living, working, eating, and playing (including a theater and bowling alley), functions that modern American life had tended to separate. Goldberg rebelled against the modernist canon, with its emphasis on the rectilinear. The rooms are pie-shaped, the balconies semicircular. "I wanted to get people out of boxes," which are really "psychological slums," he said. He likened Marina City to a "curvilinear flower form," each apartment a petal emanating from the stem.

EQUITABLE BUILDING, 1965

Skidmore, Owings & Merrill

Critics have long claimed that glass-box architecture ignores the urban environment. Perhaps by way of response, Skidmore, Owings & Merrill conceived the Equitable Building (near right, on river) to emphasize outdoor as well as indoor space. The project began when the Tribune Company, which owned the land, agreed to sell only if the new building featured a riverfront plaza. Thus, SOM built a two-story terrace with a broad, inviting spiral staircase between the street level and a walkway beside the river. The architects' minimalist touch would be worth little were it not for the balanced proportions of windows, bays, and the building's full mass, as well as rich use of travertine and bronze-tinted glass.

River Cottages, 1988

Harry Weese and Associates

Harry Weese was always something of an iconoclast, an architect who resisted prevailing trends. When the River Cottages complex was conceived in the 1980s, the decision to site townhouses on the river might have seemed preposterous. But today, amid an urban renaissance that places premium value on once-neglected riverfront property, new residential communities are growing up throughout this part of Chicago, filling in a formerly industrial zone.

57

RIVER CITY, 1986

Bertrand Goldberg Associates

Goldberg was an idealist as well as a dissenter. River City, an idea born in 1968 but not realized until 1986, represents an attempt to create a city within a city, a unified complex embracing all the facilities and amenities of urban living. Its serpentine form, initially planned to extend a half-mile in length, conforms to the river. Goldberg's curves are functional and symbolic; unlike boxes, a circle has a center, a focus that draws people together. As a practical matter, circular forms also provide a greater range of views, down the river and toward the city's inner core.

What River City residents see is a lively and panoramic view that includes Holabird and Root's Art Deco-style Chicago Board of Trade (1930) and the gabled, postmodernist 190 South LaSalle Street (1987) by architects John Burgee and Philip Johnson.

R. R. Donnelley Center, 1992

Ricardo Bofill Arquitectura with DeStefano & Partners

Leo Burnett Building, 1989

Kevin Roche–John Dinkeloo & Associates with Shaw & Associates

In the 1980s, postmodernism was the broadly applied term for a style that reached into the past for inspiration. Glass-box modernism had run its course, and architects gravitated to historical roots—sometimes a mixture of roots. In the R. R. Donnelley Center (right) the essential desired effect is lightness and glassy transparency. The elements evoking ancient Greek temples are not frivolous decoration but a statement that classical proportion can enhance all architecture, regardless of its size or date. The building's large marble lobby, featuring shallow pools and bamboo hummocks, offers further signs that architecture can enhance our lives.

In the Leo Burnett Building, the postmodernist gaze focuses on the old Chicago School. The structure is conceived as a classic Sullivanesque skyscraper—with base, shaft, and capital formed as three distinct elements—and walls of granite symbolizing the heavy masonry walls of the old Loop. Kevin Roche, an Irish-born architect, was broadly influenced by Chicago in this skyscraper, which also bears ornamental touches of Frank Lloyd Wright and the horizon-hugging architecture of the Prairie School.

333 WEST WACKER DRIVE, 1983

Kohn Pedersen Fox

Even though "outsiders" from New York designed it, this delicate glass tower has joined a handful of others on the riverfront as one of Chicago's favorite buildings. It proves that the most daunting limitations—here, an irregular site—often result in wonderfully original solutions. Its green-glass curtain wall curves with the bend in the river. Its Loop-facing side, on the other hand, forms right angles that follow the urban grid. Details large and small endow 333 West Wacker with sculptural elegance. The green tint of the glass echoes the color of the river and also reflects an abstract cityscape against the sky. The skyscraper has a capital, in the Sullivanesque tradition, but it is simply a broad glass plane, a vertical "blade" emphasizing that this building is divided down the middle, with one side oriented toward the sweeping river and the other toward the city's dense core.

CITICORP CENTER, 1987

Murphy/Jahn

In Citicorp Center, a postmodern version of a streamlined skyscraper, power resides not in composition so much as in modern materials and visual effects. This building's cascading setbacks appear to be modeled after 1920s architecture—Saarinen's unbuilt Tribune Tower, for instance, or the Daily News Building, which is next door. But the impressiveness of Helmut Jahn's glass tower mainly derives from its height, its shimmering glass walls, and inside, an almost vertiginous escalator that rises through the spacious light-filled atrium to the commuter-rail platforms above.

The riverside east of the Michigan Avenue Bridge has always been special. Before Chicago was settled it was under water, and until recently, with a few notable exceptions, it was underdeveloped. A building boom in the area sometimes known as River East began some twenty-five years ago. Since then, it has helped make the river a vital artery in the life of the city.

First to be developed was the south bank, reclaimed from the lake a century ago by the Illinois Central Railroad. For decades, the railroad jealously guarded its property rights, and commercial development was unknown in this area until after World War II, with the Prudential Building built in 1952. In the late 1960s, the railroad formed a joint venture with developers who then embarked on one of the largest urban developments ever undertaken. The 83-acre tract was planned primarily by the Office of Mies van der Rohe. After Mies died in 1969, his successor firm of Fujikawa, Conterato, Lohan & Associates served as architects for the Illinois Center complex, built up mostly in the 1970s.

On the north bank along this stretch of the river, inertia and other obstacles impeded development until the 1980s. Most of this land was owned by the Chicago Dock and Canal Trust, created in the 1850s by Chicago's first mayor, William Ogden, to control what was called the Sands—natural landfill that grew as sand built up on the windward side of the river's mouth.

For a century, Dock and Canal Trust property consisted mostly of train spurs and harbor slips.

There was little incentive to develop the land, partly because access to it was limited. In 1937, the Roosevelt Memorial Bridge completed the last link of Lake Shore Drive. While this might have increased the value of its holdings, the Trust resisted the bridge as planned and showed little interest in development beyond newsprint warehouses for the *Tribune* and the Curtiss candy factory in what is now North Pier.

The irresistible catalyst for development of some 60 acres came with the Columbus Street bridge, completed in 1982. A partnership between the Trust and the Equitable Life Assurance Society had been assembled with land and capital to create a city within a city. With a master plan devised by architect Dirk Lohan, it took the name of Cityfront Center.

A riverfront renaissance had begun elsewhere along the river, and with the active involvement of Friends of the Chicago River, plans were made to develop an elaborate Riverwalk along the north bank. It is an amenity that might have been neglected had Cityfront been developed sooner. But now, after almost two decades and the expenditure of $3 billion, Cityfront Center has become a vital nucleus for the future of Chicago, with the river its indispensable feature.

North Pier Terminal, 1905–1920

Christian A. Eckstorm
(renovated 1990, Booth/Hansen & Associates)

The exterior of North Pier Terminal, constructed between 1905 and 1920, was commonplace: brick walls, rows of windows, and pyramidal towers to relieve the monotony. But the interior featured abundant free-span space to house large furniture showrooms and warehouses alike. When developers renovated the building for commercial and retail use in the 1980s, architects from the office of Booth/Hansen took advantage of this openness to create a series of flowing spaces that open out onto the Ogden Slip wharf.

NAVY PIER, 1916

Charles Frost
(renovated 1990–1994, Benjamin Thompson and VOA Associates)

Navy Pier (left) was inspired by Daniel Burnham's 1909 Plan of Chicago, which called for the building of two long piers as part of a symmetrical grand design for the lakefront. One was constructed; Municipal Pier, as it was originally called, was built with extensive docking and elaborate recreational facilities. Designed by the Beaux-Arts architect Charles Frost, it had freight facilities plus a dance and music pavilion at its far end. Renamed Navy Pier in 1927 to honor World War I veterans, it also served pleasure steamers and hosted trade shows. During World War II, it was a training center for the U.S. Navy. From 1946 to 1965 it functioned as the Chicago campus of the University of Illinois. When the university moved out, the structure fell into disuse. The city began renovating it in 1976.

Three thousand feet long, Navy Pier rests upon timber pilings, steel tie rods, and concrete walls—all of which are invisible. Its most stunning feature is its concert hall, with its domed 100-foot-high ceiling, supported with exposed, half-arched radial steel trusses. "Venetian" towers bear touches of Renaissance, Gothic, and indigenous Prairie School architecture. The Crystal Garden, added as part of the recent renovation, is inspired by the vast glass exposition halls erected in London and Paris in the mid-nineteenth century. The pier's new Ferris wheel evokes the World's Columbian Exposition of 1893. And the 1995 Skyline Stage, with its fabric roof wrapped over a steel superstructure, is unique in Chicago.

NBC TOWER, 1989

Skidmore, Owings & Merrill

Among the most distinguished and visible Chicago skyscrapers of the 1980s, NBC Tower was designed by Adrian Smith of Skidmore, Owings & Merrill. Reflecting the firm's transition away from pure modernism, it also represents corporate America's renewed taste for buildings with substantial stone exteriors and richly finished interiors, not to mention easy pedestrian access to the surrounding environment. In addition, with its soaring vertical piers and series of setbacks, the structure bears a resemblance to Art Deco skyscrapers in Chicago and New York, including NBC's Rockefeller Center. "Cities, especially great architectural cities, are built over a long time span," said Smith, "and there is usually a great deal of respect between generations of architects." NBC Tower is a demonstration of such respect.

HYATT REGENCY HOTEL, 1974–1980

A. Epstein and Sons

TWO ILLINOIS CENTER, 1973

Office of Mies van der Rohe

THREE ILLINOIS CENTER, 1980

Fujikawa, Conterato, Lohan & Associates

When Mies van der Rohe began drawing up plans for the site where the Hyatt Regency Hotel and Illinois Center now stand, he was working on a clean slate; the land had been a rail yard and had never been built upon. Mies imagined a complex of modern skyscrapers rising on the edge of the Loop, graced with open plazas and enclosed walkways. He and various protégés planned the buildings of Illinois Center, and the local firm of A. Epstein and Sons designed the Hyatt Regency (front center, with towers behind and to the right). Juxtaposed with the towering Aon Center (formerly Standard Oil of Indiana Building, then Amoco Building), designed by Edward Durrell Stone with Perkins & Will in 1974, the entire complex comprises an expansive city within a city.

SHERATON CHICAGO HOTEL AND TOWERS, 1992

Solomon Cordwell Buenz and Associates

As the development of Cityfront Center got under way, Chicago's postmodernist architects looked to the city's architectural past for inspiration. The firm of Solomon, Cordwell, Buenz and Associates found it in Louis Sullivan's Carson Pirie Scott building (1904), among the most graceful of the old Chicago School. Like the store on State Street, the Sheraton's corner tower features the touch of a tall building, while its strong horizontal lines play off the new Riverwalk, which passes along the length of the hotel.

LAKE POINT TOWER, 1968

George Schipporeit and John Heinrich

NORTH PIER APARTMENTS, 1991

Dubin, Dubin & Moutoussamy

The curved form of Lake Point Tower (right) evokes one of Mies van der Rohe's most visionary unbuilt projects, a glass tower for Berlin whose transparency and play of light fascinated German architects. George Schipporeit and John Heinrich, who had been students of Mies, recalled that project when asked to design an apartment building that should feature, above all, as many unbroken views of Lake Michigan as possible. The apartments (now condominiums) were equipped with movable walls, enabling residents to change floor plans or combine apartments as needed.

Lake Point Tower was the last private structure built before a lakefront ordinance was amended to ensure that all land east of Lake Shore Drive would remain "forever open, clear, and free." But building close to the lakefront remains irresistible, and the North Pier Apartments (left) are pressed up against Lake Shore Drive, resulting in splendid views but unfortunate congestion at street level.

CENTENNIAL FOUNTAIN, 1989

Lohan Associates

Architect Dirk Lohan's office designed the fountain and water cannon to celebrate the centennial of the founding of the Chicago Sanitary District, the governmental body that succeeded in reversing the flow of the river. "I wanted to symbolize the natural phenomenon of water," said Lohan, "how it comes from one source, spreads, and goes back to another." The Vermont granite fountain and the 80-foot arch across the river also signify the impact that the hand of humankind can have on water, in this case very much for the better.

GLEACHER CENTER, 1994

Lohan Associates

Gleacher Center houses the University of Chicago's Graduate School of Business. One objective of the design was to forge a downtown identity for the university. Another aim was to improve the area for pedestrians along this stretch of Riverfront Center. Gleacher Center harks back to several architectural models. Its stylized masonry facade echoes the Gothic-revival buildings of the university's century-old campus in Hyde Park. Its expansive walls of glass and steel evoke the modernism of Mies van der Rohe, who was architect Dirk Lohan's grandfather. The five-story atrium inside recalls the great central atriums of the Chicago School, which valued natural light almost as much as rentable space.

BLUE CROSS-BLUE SHIELD BUILDING, 1996

Lohan Associates

AON CENTER, 1973

Edward Durrell Stone with Perkins & Will

These skyscrapers illustrate how much architectural tastes can change within a single generation. The Blue Cross–Blue Shield Building (center), designed by Lohan Associates, features great expanses of glass—trimmed with substantial granite piers—that provide office workers with wonderful views. Amazingly, this thirty-story building was designed so that as many as twenty-four floors can be added to it.

The eighty-story Aon Center, as it is now called (second from right), was built as the headquarters of Standard Oil of Indiana and later became the Amoco Building. It was for a brief time after its completion the world's tallest building. Its original design combined boxlike modernism with a sheathing composed of one of the earth's most venerable building materials, Carrara marble. Disastrously, the marble panels surrendered to the cold and just a few years after completion were in danger of falling off. The entire exterior was reclad in granite at a cost of between $60 and $80 million, nearly the original cost of the building.

CHICAGO RIVER LOCKS, 1938

U. S. Army Corps of Engineers

ROOSEVELT MEMORIAL BRIDGE, 1937

Strauss Engineering with Hugh Young

The Army Corps of Engineers built the lock chamber at the mouth of the Chicago River to address complaints, perhaps unfounded, that the reversal of the river's flow in 1900 had lowered the level of Lake Michigan. The Lake Shore Drive (or Roosevelt Memorial) Bridge was the result of a hard-won political accord between the South Park and Lincoln Park commissions, then separate taxing bodies, to connect their two sections of Chicago's lakefront boulevard. This is a double-deck, double-leaf bascule bridge, featuring modernist bridge houses designed in the setback style of streamlined skyscrapers downtown.

Swissôtel, 1989

Harry Weese and Associates

Three Illinois Center, 1980

Fujikawa, Conterato, Lohan & Associates

If the late Harry Weese seems to have been obsessed with triangles (he used them constantly), it may be because he was intent on breaking free of the right-angle orthodoxy of modernism. Here, the triangle accomplishes something important for the interior—providing good views of Lake Michigan for a great number of rooms—as it does for the glimmering and conspicuous exterior. The forty-three-story hotel stands in sharp contrast to the stark modernism of Three Illinois Center, by Fujikawa, Conterato, Lohan & Associates, direct heirs to the legacy of Mies van der Rohe.

Index of Architects

INDEX OF BUILDINGS

INDEX

CREDITS

Montgomery Ward Bldgs.

Chicago Tribune Printing Plant

LaSalle Street (140 W)

Chicago Avenue (800 N)

Delaware Place (900 N)

Chestnut Street (860 N)

Pearson Street (830 N)

John Hancock Center

Superior Street (732 N)

Wells Street (200 W)

Clark Street (100 W)

Dearborn Street (35 W)

State Street (0 W)

Wabash Avenue (44 E)

Rush Street (65 E)

N. Michigan Ave (100E)

Fairbanks Court (300 E)

McClurg Court (400 E)

Huron Street (700 N)

Erie Street (658 N)

St. Claire Street (200 E)

Ontario Street (628 N)

Ohio Street (600 N)

Apparel Center

Merchandise Mart

Helene Curtis Bldg.

City Parking Garage

Reid, Murdoch & Co. Bldg.

Westin River North Hotel

Quaker Tower

Grand Avenue (530 N)

Marina City

Chicago Sun-Times

IBM Bldg.

Lincoln Tower

333 N. Michigan Ave.

One Illinois Center

Wrigley Bldg.

Tribune Tower

U of C Gleacher Center

Equitable Bldg.

NBC Tower

Sheraton Chicago Hotel

Centennial Fountain

No

Illinois Street (500 N)

Chicago River

River Cottages

Chicago River

Hubbard Street (430 N)

Kinzie Street (400 N)

225 W. Wacker Drive

333 W. Wacker Drive

165 N. Canal

Wacker Drive (340 N)

Lake Street (200 N)

Boeing World Headquarters

Three Illinois Center

Swissôtel

Columbus Plaza

Hyatt Regency Hotel

Two Illinois Center

London Guarantee Bldg.

Hotel 71

17th Church of Christ, Scientist

Jeweler's Bldg.

One East Wacker Drive

Stouffer's Hotel

Leo Burnett Bldg.

55 W. Wacker Dr.

R.R. Donnelley Center

LaSalle-Wacker Bldg.

Builders Bldg. Addition

Builders Bldg.

Engineering Building

211 W. Wacker Dr.

Great Lakes Building

150 N. Wacker Dr.

123 N. Wacker Dr.

Old Morton Bldg.

101 N. Wacker Dr.

Aon Center

Blue Cross-Blue Shield B

Daily News Bldg.
(One N. Riverside Plaza)

Northwestern Atrium Center

Randolph Street (150 N)

Washington Street (100 N)

90

Madison Street (0 N)

94

Monroe Street (100 S)

Gateway Center I & II

222 S. Riverside Plaza

Mid-America
Commodities Exch.

Gateway Center IV

Old Post Office

Adams Street (200 S)

Jackson Boulevard (300 S)

Van Buren Street (400 S)

Canal Street (500 W)

Wacker Dr. (360 W)

Franklin Street (300 W)

Civic Opera Building

One S. Wacker Dr.

10-30 S. Wacker Dr.

100 S. Wacker Dr.

150 S. Wacker Dr.

200 S. Wacker Dr.

Sears Tower

250 S. Wacker Dr.

300 S. Wacker Dr.

311 S. Wacker Dr.

Michigan Avenue (100 E)

Columbus Drive (301 E)

Lake Shore Drive

Congress Parkway (500 S)

Harrison Street (600 S)

DesPlaines Street (630 W)

Jefferson Street (600 W)

Clinton Street (540 W)

Canal Street (500 W)

New Post Office

Chicago River

Polk Street (800 S)

Chicago River

River City

Taylor Street (1000 S)

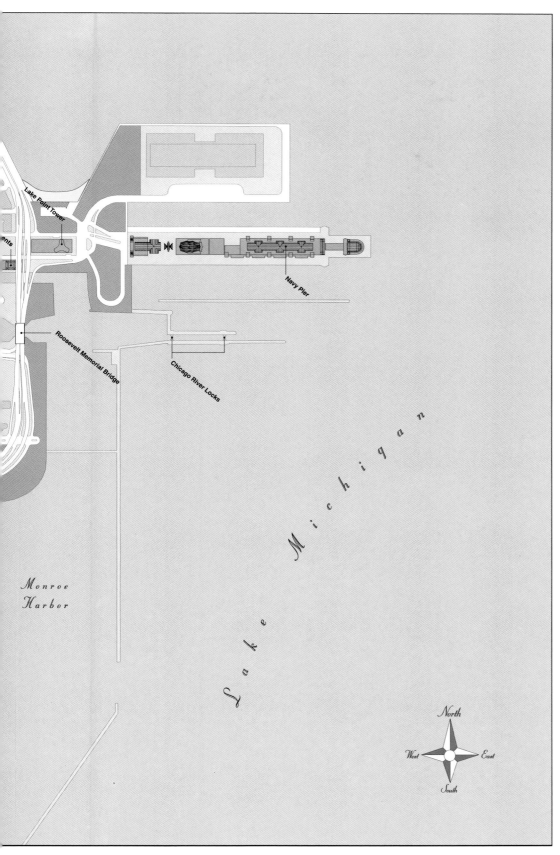

95